THE FINAL TRIUMPH

A One-Act
Easter Chancel Drama
BY J. B. QUISENBERRY

C.S.S Publishing Co., Inc.
Lima, Ohio

THE FINAL TRIUMPH

9211 / ISBN 1-55673-395-X   PRINTED IN U.S.A.

To Claude and Kate, for
their patience and their love.

INTRODUCTION

This service requires period costumes, which may range from simple bath robes to realistic period pieces. The setting is simple.

The drama is actually a short one-act play and does require blocking and memorization. The cast for this drama is quite small.

The music is a suggestion, and may be changed. All music may be sung by a choir, congregation, soloists or any combination of the three.

The service is easy to produce and offers the opportunity for lay people of various ages to be involved. Production time is about 50 minutes.

THE FINAL TRIUMPH

A Service For Easter
A Chancel Drama In One Act

PLAY CAST

Annas . . . . Priest of the Temple
old, wise

Caiaphas . . . . Priest
hot tempered

Mary Magdalene . . . . Follower of Jesus
young, angry

Mary, Mother of Jesus . . . . Old
wise, serene

Guard 1

Guard 2

SETTING

The temple in Jerusalem on Easter morning. As the play begins, Annas sits in a chair center stage reading a scroll. Caiaphas enters from the back of the sanctuary, very upset, and proceeds up the center aisle toward Annas.

The two priests should be wearing rich looking robes in contrast to the plainer costumes of the two women. Choir robes work very well for the priest costumes. They should also both wear ornate skullcaps.

,

ORDER OF SERVICE

PRELUDE

INTROIT

CALL TO WORSHIP

L. Rejoice! The Lord is risen!

P. He is risen indeed!

L. The Pharisees and the Romans thought they had defeated him.

P. They did not have the power.

L. Neither the powers of earth nor the powers of Hell could defeat our Lord.

P. He is risen! We are free!

HYMN OF PRAISE "Sing With All The Sons of Glory"

CALL TO PRAYER

L. The Lord be with you.

P. And also with you.

L. Let us pray.

PRAYER *(In Unison)*

Almighty and everlasting God, who through your dear Son defeated death, and opened the gates of heaven for all those who believe in him; grant that we too, as we celebrate his resurrection, may be reborn through your grace. Fill us with your eternal Spirit Lord, so that we might be new creatures in thee, set free from the cares of this world by the knowledge that we, through the love of Christ, may live eternally. In the name of him who died and rose again we pray. Amen.

PASTORAL PRAYER

LORD'S PRAYER

11

L. I will extol you, O Lord, for you have lifted me up, and did not let my foes rejoice over me.

P. O Lord my God, I cried to you for help, and you healed me.

L. O Lord, you brought up my soul from Sheol,

P. Restored me to life from among those gone down to the pit.

L. Sing praises to the Lord, O His faithful ones, and give thanks to his holy name.

P. Surely the Lord's anger is but for a moment; the Lord's favor is for a lifetime.

L. Weeping may tarry for the night, but joy comes with the morning.

P. As for me, I said in my prosperity, "I shall never be moved."

L. By your favor, O Lord, you had established me as a strong mountain;

P. You hid your face, I was dismayed.

L. To you, O Lord, I cried, and to the Lord I made supplication:

P. "What profit is there in my death, if I go down to the pit?

L. Will the dust praise you? Will it tell of your faithfulness?

P. Hear, O Lord, and be gracious to me! O Lord, be my helper!"

L. You have turned my mourning into dancing; you have loosed my sackcloth and girded me with gladness, that my soul may praise you and not be silent.

P. O Lord, my God, I will give thanks to you forever.

GLORIA PATRI

FIRST LESSON Isaiah 25:6-9

ANTHEM "I Know That My Redeemer Liveth" by G. F. Handel

SECOND LESSON 1 Peter 1:3-9

OFFERTORY

DOXOLOGY

HYMN OF PRAISE "Crown Him With Many Crowns"

GOSPEL LESSON John 20:1-18

WITNESS TO THE WORD

THE FINAL TRIUMPH One-Act

HYMN OF PRAISE "Jesus Christ Is Risen Today"

BENEDICTION

POSTLUDE

THE FINAL TRIUMPH

(Annas enters right, arranges a chair center stage, sits in it and begins to read a scroll.)

CAIAPHAS: *(Entering from the back of the sanctuary, very excited.)* There you are! Don't you know? The whole city is in an uproar!

ANNAS: *(Calmly)* Of course it is Caiaphas. It's Passover. The city is always crowded this time of year. Jerusalem is full of pilgrims.

13

CAIAPHAS: No Lord Annas, the city is full of fanatics! The followers of that carpenter's son are everywhere!

ANNAS: Calm yourself son-in-law. *(Annas stands and puts his hand on Caiaphas' shoulder.)* Just last night you were laughing at what cowards these people are. You couldn't get over the way that they all deserted their leader when he was tried and crucified. You said that they were comical.

CAIAPHAS: *(Turning away from Annas and crossing down right)* Yes! I know what I said! But that was last night. This morning is a different thing all together! *(He turns back to face Annas.)* These people are everywhere, shouting and singing and claiming that the old prophecy has been fulfilled!

ANNAS: *(Sitting back down)* What prophecy is that?

CAIAPHAS: *(Crossing to Annas)* The one that says that the Messiah will rise from the dead three days after his death.

ANNAS: *(After a short pause)* But isn't the Nazarene's body in the tomb?

CAIAPHAS: No!

ANNAS: *(Standing)* No?

CAIAPHAS: The tomb stands empty.

ANNAS: That's impossible!

CAIAPHAS: *(Paces down right)* Impossible or not, true or not, that is what these fanatics are saying. And what's more, *(He turns to face Annas.)* people are beginning to believe them! The danger of revolution is greater now, with the Nazarene dead, than it was when he was alive!

14

ANNAS: But what has happened to the body? Didn't Joseph and Nicodemus bury it Friday night? Have the old weasels tricked us? *(He sits.)*

CAIAPHAS: No. I saw them take the body myself, and my spies watched as the old fools and a few women buried him as though he were a faithful Jew. They laid him in the tomb Joseph had prepared for himself. *(During this speech, he crosses back to Annas.)*

ANNAS: And the great stone, was it placed securely?

CAIAPHAS: *(Nodding)* Not only that, but I personally asked Pilate to place the Seal of Rome across it and post guards at the tomb to prevent anyone from stealing the body.

ANNAS: And Pilate agreed? *(Caiaphas nods.)* Then what happened?

CAIAPHAS: How should I know! *(He crosses down right.)* But something must be done! Now! Those fools who followed Jesus are telling fantastic stories all over the city. *(He turns back toward Annas.)* Something must be done before we lose control!

ANNAS: Calm yourself Caiaphas. Hysteria will get us nowhere. We can not control others, if we ourselves lose control.

(A commotion is heard at the back of the sanctuary. Two guards enter with two women. Mary Magdalene is yelling and struggling with one of the guards as he forces her to walk down the center aisle toward the Priests. Mary walks behind them quietly with the other guard.)

ANNAS: *(Standing)* What is this? What is the meaning of this?

15

GUARD #1: We beg your pardon Lord Annas. *(Both guards bow.)* Lord Caiaphas sent orders to bring in as many of the Nazarene's followers as we could find for questioning.

ANNAS: I see. *(He scowls at Caiaphas, then turns to Mary Magdalene who is still struggling with Guard #2.)* Young woman! Young woman! This is God's house! Be still in his presence! *(She calms down.)* You have nothing to fear from me. We only want to ask you a few questions. *(To the guards)* I think you can let go of them now. *(The guards let go of the women and stand one to the right and one to the left of the communion rail. They should stand "at ease," and out of the way of the main action, but still in sight.)*

CAIAPHAS: *(Advancing on Mary Magdalene.)* Where is it? Where have you hidden the body? *(Mary Magdalene snickers, which makes Caiaphas furious.)* What are you laughing at you little fool! Don't you realize what we could do to you?

MARY MAGDALENE: Oh, I know what you are capable of Lord Caiaphas. It's just that your question is the same one that I asked the gardener at the tomb this morning. You see, I thought that you had ordered my Lord's body removed in order to defile it.

CAIAPHAS: Then it was this gardener who started these lies! Tell us his name. He will pay dearly for it!

ANNAS: Please, Lord Caiaphas, get a hold of yourself. Now tell me young woman, *(To Mary Magdalene)* what is your name, and what was your relationship to the Nazarene? *(Annas is very calm, unlike Caiaphas.)*

MARY MAGDALENE: They call me Mary Magdalene, and I have followed my Lord ever since he saved me from being stoned to death for adultery. He came up to me, and . . .

CAIAPHAS: An adulteress! You see the kind of people this man had following him?

ANNAS: *(Scowling at Caiaphas)* Caiaphas! I see, *(To Mary Magdalene)* but what concerns us right now is what has happened this morning. Could you tell us?

MARY MAGDALENE: We were going to the tomb to finish the rites of the dead. There was so little time before the sun set Friday. We were worried that the soldiers would not let us into the tomb, but as we turned the corner of the path, we saw that the soldiers were gone. The tomb was empty! When I realized that the tomb was empty, I was beside myself. I was afraid that you or Pilate had had my Lord's body removed in order to defile it. I was frightened and confused. I ran into the garden, sank to the ground, and began to weep. I have never felt so alone.

CAIAPHAS: *(Impatiently)* Yes! Yes! So you were beside yourself, but what about the gardener? Where does he come in? Get to the point woman!

ANNAS: Patience, Lord Caiaphas. Go on my dear. Lord Caiaphas is a bit upset. He means you no harm.

MARY MAGDALENE: *(Challenging Caiaphas)* He doesn't scare me anymore. None of you scare me! My Lord lives! You have lost False Priest.

CAIAPHAS: *(Starting toward her in a rage)* I'll have your impertinent tongue torn from your head! You . . .

ANNAS: *(Stopping Caiaphas with an out-stretched hand)* Please son-in-law! Restrain yourself! Now Mary, continue your story, but with a bit more respect. We are the Priests of the Lord God, and you are in his holy temple.

17

MARY MAGDALENE: Yes, well as I was saying, I sat in the garden crying. I was suddenly aware of someone near me. When I turned around, I saw a man standing over me. I thought that he was the gardener. It was still very early for people to be up and about. I was sure that he would know where they had taken the body, so I begged him to tell me. *(She turns away from the priests, lost in her memory.)* Even though I was shouting at him, the man remained quiet. Then he smiled at me, and called my name. For a moment I was confused. How would this man know my name? Then he said my name again, and I saw that it wasn't the gardener at all, but the Lord, alive again! I reached out to embrace him, but he stepped back. "Touch me not," he said, "I have not yet ascended to my Father. Go tell the disciples that I am risen." *(She pauses to savor the moment, then turns to Caiaphas.)* So you see my Lords, he has beaten you! Even death can not hold him! You have lost as he said that you would!

(Caiaphas starts toward her, but Annas stops him with a look.)

ANNAS: You saw Jesus of Nazareth alive this morning? Did anyone else see him?

MARY MAGDALENE: No. I told you that I was alone.

ANNAS: And you did not actually touch him?

MARY MAGDALENE: He told me not to. What are you trying to say?

ANNAS: You were alone, upset, overcome with grief, perhaps your mind . . .

MARY MAGDALENE: No! No! I saw him! I talked to him!

ANNAS: The mind can do strange things sometimes, especially when one is under stress.

MARY MAGDALENE: *(Very upset)* No! I saw him! I talked to him! I . . .

MARY: *(Putting her arm around Mary Magdalene)* Sh, my child. Don't let them upset you. You know the truth. Sh. Sh.

CAIAPHAS: *(Triumphantly crossing up right)* Ha! So that's it! All this uproar over the ravings of a demented woman! And we were worried!

ANNAS: *(Ignoring Caiaphas)* Who are you madam? *(To Mary)*

MARY: I am his mother.

CAIAPHAS: The Nazarene's?

MARY: Yes.

ANNAS: I see. But you are so calm amid all of this chaos. Could it be that you do not believe this young woman's story?

MARY: On the contrary, I know that it is true.

ANNAS: How?

MARY: Many times my Son told me that he would rise from the dead. Why should I doubt it now that it has happened?

ANNAS: You believe her story then?

MARY: Yes.

ANNAS: Have you seen your Son this morning?

MARY: No.

ANNAS: Then when did you hear this news?

MARY: I knew within myself long before we saw the empty tomb and the angel.

ANNAS: Angel?

MARY: Yes. An angel appeared to us after Mary had left. The angel told us that Jesus had risen from the dead, just as he had said that he would.

CAIAPHAS: Bah! More hysterical women's dribble! Surely my Lord . . .

ANNAS: *(Ignoring Caiaphas)* And what did you do then?

MARY: We rushed to tell Peter and the others what we had seen, but Mary, being younger, was already there by the time that we arrived.

ANNAS: You keep saying "us" and "we." Were there others with you?

MARY: Yes, there were four of us originally, but Mary ran away as she has told you.

ANNAS: And did these other women see the angel, too?

MARY: Oh yes. We all saw the angel, and heard his message.

ANNAS: And did Peter and the other disciples believe your story?

MARY: They were stunned and confused at first, but after both I and Mary had told our stories as you call them, John and Peter rushed to the tomb. They saw the angel, too. They are spreading the news all over the city as we speak.

MARY MAGDALENE: *(To Caiaphas)* Soon all of Jerusalem will know that you have lost Priests!

CAIAPHAS: *(He starts toward her, but Annas stops him.)* You'll follow your Master to Golgotha, you . . .

MARY: My Son once said, Lord Caiaphas, that should all of our voices be silenced, the stones themselves would rise up to shout his praises. So you see, Mary is right. You have lost. What man, however mighty, can win against God? You killed him. Yes. He died on that cross you nailed him to Friday, but my Son has risen! Deny it if you wish. Punish us all for our faith, but, in the end, it will be the same. You have lost! My Son lives! That, my Lords, is the truth, whether you believe it or not!

CAIAPHAS: I've had enough of this stupidity! Guards, take them away to prison!

ANNAS: You forget yourself son-in-law! I am the Elder here!

CAIAPHAS: Forgive me, my Lord.

ANNAS: Guards, take these women out and release them.

CAIAPHAS: Release them? Are you mad!

ANNAS: *(To the guards who are now standing beside the women)* You have your orders.

(Guards and women exit.)

CAIAPHAS: I can't believe you let those women go! An example must be made! These stories must be stopped!

ANNAS: I have never seen you so upset Caiaphas. Could it be that you are afraid of a dead man?

CAIAPHAS: Bah! It's his fanatic followers that scare me! They should scare you, too! They will bring a revolution and the wrath of Rome down upon our heads! My God Annas! How can you be so calm? Do something!

ANNAS: *(Sitting)* What would you have me do, Caiaphas? Kill them all?

CAIAPHAS: Yes! . . . No. That shouldn't be necessary. Surely one or two more crucifixions will cool their zeal. We only have to scare them, and they'll stop this insanity.

ANNAS: Scare them? We scared them when we killed their leader. But they aren't afraid anymore! You still don't understand, do you son-in-law?

CAIAPHAS: Even fanatics want to live. If they realize that their faith means death, they'll . . .

ANNAS: Don't you think they know that alreadyl? Those women just now, they knew what they were risking, but they weren't afraid. After last Friday, they all know what they risk.

CAIAPHAS: But that's insane!

ANNAS: Perhaps, but they believe that their leader has risen from the dead, and they all expect to do the same. Your threats don't frighten them anymore Caiaphas.

CAIAPHAS: But these tales of rising from the dead are impossible! Something must be done to stop them! They threaten us all!

ANNAS: *(Standing)* Do what you want. I'm tired. I need to rest. But Caiaphas, be careful. God only knows where this all will end. *(Annas starts down the center aisle, but then turns back to face Caiaphas.)* I'm terrified that we have made an awful mistake, we and our powerful friends who are afraid of the truth. *(He starts back down the aisle.)*

CAIAPHAS: What is the truth? Do you know? *(Annas turns)*

ANNAS: No, but it may have been truth himself that we crucified and buried Friday, but truth, as usual, rose again. *(He continues down the aisle.)*

CAIAPHAS: Wait! What are you talking about? I don't understand!

ANNAS: Nor do I, Caiaphas. *(Annas turns to face Caiaphas who is standing in front of the chair, center.)* But I'm afraid those women were right. The Nazarene said it himself as he hung on that cross we nailed him to Friday. "It is finished." I'm afraid that the final triumph is his, and there is nothing that you, or I, or all the powers of Hell can do about it. *(He starts back down the aisle.)*

CAIAPHAS: But Lord Annas! I don't . . .

ANNAS: *(His back to Caiaphas, still walking toward the back of the sanctuary)* I'm going to bed. Do what you will.

(Annas exits at the back of the sanctuary. Caiaphas stands for a moment looking after him, then storms off right.)